Spreading the Bad Word

Also by Dominic Kirwan and published by Ginninderra Press
Miracles Become Monsters
Put a Smile On That Face
Where Words Go When They Die
The Holy Babble
The Mouth in the Sky

Dominic Kirwan

Spreading the Bad Word

Thank yous

'Beautiful:
Being a Joke to People Who Don't Usually Laugh.'
– Dominic Kirwan

I would like to thank the Void, for staring back, laughing at my bad jokes, and just being there for me.

I would also like to thank Lee (Ninja) for his support and friendship.

Other notable mentions: Peter Gate, Sally Harbison, Leonie Hagstrom, Troy Dean, Trevor Thirkettle and my wonderful mother, Barbara.

Spreading the Bad Word
ISBN 978 1 76109 682 2
Copyright © text Dominic Kirwan 2024
Cover image: *Two Messiahs* by Kim Loudon

First published 2024 by
GINNINDERRA PRESS
PO Box 3461 Port Adelaide 5015
www.ginninderrapress.com.au

Contents

Part 1
- Unseize the Day — 9
- Downloading God — 12
- Don't Write About Love — 15
- Don't Answer the Door — 17
- Mother — 20
- Shadow — 21
- A Line-up of Romantic Criminals — 23
- And As the Silent Terror Grips Me — 27
- You Are in a Movie Without Cameras — 29
- The Roadie and the Rock Star — 31

Part 2
- The Church of Nothing — 35
- Gratitude — 39
- Minefield — 41
- Repentagram — 42
- Mary Begs for an Abortion — 45
- Requiem Cliché — 48
- Punched in the Face by Gandhi — 50
- Nonsense, said the Drunk — 53
- Le Petite Mort (ification) — 55
- A Church Without Windows — 57

Part 3
- The Exorcism was a Thundering Success — 61
- A Lonely Old Man — 64
- An Unattended Funeral — 66
- Creeping Jesus — 68
- Smiley Face — 72
- Sunday — 75

An Illuminated Light Bulb	76
The Fear	79
A Hopeless Romantic Reading Poetry to the Dead	80
Bad Actor	81

Part 4

Cheers	87
Tequila Mockingbird	89
Don't Kill Yourself, Just Kiss Me	90
You Are Necessary	91
Unlucky Stars	94
Deathstination	96
The Medication Vending Machines Are Empty	99
The Last Resort	101
Im(mortality)	106
Your Ghost	110

Part 5

Knickers	115
The Eroticisation of a Hyper Reality TV Food Disorder	117
Gehenna	120
Love Sickness Uber Alles	123
Spiders and Vampires	125
The Freedom from Information Act	128
Insert Coin	130
Sell Me Why I'm Here	134
The Power of Disco	136
I'm Thinking of Leaving You	138

Part 1

Unseize the Day

A haemorrhaging black heart,
Beating wildly, untamed, exploding
Splashing in puddles of children's tears
Like a clap nappy jackhammer
All safety pins and yellow diarrhoea
Celebrating destruction
In the hands of a chiselled slave
Fuelled by alcohol,
Straitjackets and pharmaceuticals
Tearing reality's concrete asunder
Blitzing out all reason

Bugged-out eyes and pregnant insects
Panicked by the teacup storm
Flying in manic circles
Smashing up against fly screens
And panes of murky glass
Repeatedly
Futility rattling like kryptonite
In a leaden jewellery box
Soulless eyes, windows screaming on display
Streaked with eye gunk, filth and desire
There is no escape from this room

A haemorrhaging mind
Raging to escape its soul cage
Trephination, lobotomy, vasectomy
Hands shaking as they wield the drill, the knife
Meant to set the demons free
A reckoning of death rattles like new wave LSD
There is no escape from this room

Pale parades on winding, bleached streets
An advertisement for anomalous sexuality
A product placement for earnt insanity
Window shopping was never this fulfilling
I am titillated by the Central Brisbane District wildlife
The animals, wielding smartphones, vegan snack foods
and retail therapy shopping bags
They have never seemed so beguiling
Beautiful women with strutting gorillas, sleeves tattooed
Fat, lard legions, mishappen pensioners,
the elderly, the wheelchair warriors,
the delightfully deformed
Drug addicts and lazy-eyed thugs in Target tracksuits
Bipolar saviours on manic marijuana,
and methamphetamine medication
All of them with God complexes
Just dying to pray over me, to save me
And bludge a cigarette I don't possess

'Got any loose change, mister?' they ask.
'Sorry. I don't carry change. Nor am I going to change,'
'you're just going to have to love me the way I am,' I reply.

I am married to a plethora of cancerous maladies
I am an invisible rock star
Taking on the world
With a drunken eye for the unseen
And a bottle of whisky in my hand

'I'll bring the bottle
And you bring the glasses
So you can see what hit ya!'

Jesus Lizards and Virginal Marys
Death Wish Kennedys and Public Housing Enemies
Santa Claus is the Devil
I am at the mercy of his presence
I am scheduled for my monthly exorcism
And a government needle

At the end of Death Valley
Buried beneath a mountain
Of writhing naked bodies
You will surely find the love
You have been searching for your whole life
Dig for it
Fuck your way to the bottom
It's waiting there for you

So, Unseize the day, pilgrim
The time is nigh
For a miracle

Downloading God

To download Purpose from this torrent site
Engage your Virtual Dream Diary
Then click here…

Imagine Anaïs Nin
Kissing Antonin Artaud
Picasso in a bar room brawl
With Vincent Van Gogh
William Shatner jelly-wrestling
Mother Theresa

Three existentialists walk into a bar
And nothing happens…
Fuck all…

Imagine Jesus in a dance-off
Against Judas Iscariot
Marilyn Monroe in a crack house
Spanking Pope Benedict
Your favourite boy band, dangling
All hanging from their necks
From a burning fig tree

'There must be a point to this shit,' he said.
'No,' I replied. 'There isn't.'

'But if you are looking for one,' I began,
And pointing with subtle emphasis at a glowing icon
In the corner of the screen
Reflected in my very own eye
That may or may not
Represent the very heart of the Internet itself
I said,
'Then you have come to the wrong place.'

To download God from this torrent site
Engage your Virtual Private Network
Then click here…

The screen fills with an image
Of Joan of Arc's frilly knickers
On fire
The room fills with smoke
The neighbour's smoke alarm goes off
Nobody does anything about it
The screen goes blank

God says,

'Sorry
The page you are attempting to access
Is either
Temporarily unavailable
Or it does not exist
It's up to you
How you process this information
Either give up entirely
Or come back later
And try again.'

Don't Write About Love

Don't write about love
Find yourself in a violent, untamed land
Find yourself broken and beaming fuck-you sunshine
Find yourself naked and gracious and sober,
White knuckled, shaking and raw
And live

Don't write about love
Drown in its rivers
Freeze in its winters
Binge on the falling snow till all feeling is gone
And your words are numb simulacrums
Of poems unwritten
Echoing like silence in frozen veins
Thirst in its deserts
Drink from eviscerated cactus
Till your mouth fills with blood
Then swallow it

Don't write about love
Live it
Climb its mountains
Throw yourself into its canyons
Shut out the voices that whisper to you,
'You don't belong here'
Jam your fingers in your ears
Till you touch cerebrum
Then keep pushing
Till your eyes well with hot oily tears

Blot out the sun for its insolence
Tear the stars from the sky for doubting you
And then tame them
Sing out of tune in the darkness
Smash the very last mirror
Then juggle the shards
Kiss the mouth in the sky
Till all you can taste is fire and ash
Walk the winding path
Until your heartbeat hammers so hard
It falls out of your chest

Don't write about love
Murder it with words
Hunt it down and haunt its bones
Worship it for its absences
Embrace it for its shattered promises
Pick your beating heart up off the ground
All the goop and sinew and soup
Place it back in your chest
Then keep on walking

And though you are weary
Somewhere on this winding pathway
There will be someone to love

Don't Answer the Door

'No love,' I say
Just distractions from madness
Just friendship and untamed memories
I am an advertisement for happy
In her company
I could get used to this

I want to eat her
Like cancer
Like dark chocolate
Swirling, malignant
Like a rough tongue lapping
Like an inchworm jiving
On a black asphalt runway

Blood milk
Trickles down her thighs
Secrets tumble like lucky dice
From her ears
The old flame flickers in our eyes
But it is blown out
Like a roman candle
We make wishes in the wax

She paints her blue eyes closed
So that I might pry them open
She smears her gills with honey
So that I might lick them clean

'No love,' she says
Just temporarily temporary conversations
About our yesterdays
As we wade,
Up to our necks in literary mud

She has such a beatific smile, I think
I am tempted to steal it
Smear it over my own face
Like a wave of wet plaster on burnt toast

'No love,' I say
Just distractions from madness
My memories hide
Beneath the oil slick
That settles like a thick layer of skin
On the surface of a crystal-clear pond

Tick tock
Knock, knock, knock

If I don't answer the door
My heart will be safe

Still, there is no stopping
The incessant knock
        knock
        knocking

The Boogie Man
A romantic monstrosity
Waiting in the unchecked cold
Outside my door

'Answer it,' she says, teasing
'I dare you.'
'No,' I reply tersely,
'Do you think I'm crazy?'
'Yep,' she says, laughing
Like she knows
Really knows
What's waiting out there
For me

Why would I let love in?
It would ruin everything

Mother

Mother, all I get from you is love
You disregard my failings
You cherish my feelings
Even if they are self-murderous

Mother, you are a vivid beating heart
A blinding light in my insufferable darkness

I want to go before you
As a world without you
Would be unbearable

Mother, I love you more than life itself

Now we walk together in the twilight
Hand in hand
Instead of being pushed in a pram
Repeating every word you said
Like a parrot soon to be poet
I am still a babe, and you are my icon
If I were a sculptor
I would forge a statue in your honour
But I am just a lowly scribe
And these are my words
Born of God

Shadow

When I raised my gaze to meet hers
I beheld a shyness
A worn-out kindness,
We had both known this passion play before
The performance, the crying crowd
I searched her eyes for tears, anything
That might give her away
That same shadow that I had seen
When I closed my own eyes
Settled upon her features, frail, broken
Tearing her secrets away
Thread by thread
Like a ratty, bloodstained carpet
Like a vermillion marriage trail
And a wedding dress
Its white lace blackened by soot
From the fire that burned
Before I knew her

Shadow
Holding us back from the light
Shadow
The secrets we share
Shadow
We are all alone in this, together

I couldn't be with her, I knew that now
Those unknowable eyes
Those milk-white thighs
The way her money
Meant nothing to me
The way kissing her lips
Led to perversonality trips
And psychopathology
I was finally a man alone, without a map
That could lead me home
Marooned, on a random island of her choosing

Would I scream
Blue bloody murder
To be with her?

No.

The tools with which she tortures hearts
Need to be taken away
Her toys, undeployed
To keep us all safe
From her beauty

We share
The same shadow
We have known this
Forever

I am so sorry
We cannot be together

A Line-up of Romantic Criminals

I was inclined
To tear your heart apart
But it simply wasn't breakable
Now you're just another silhouette
In a line-up of romantic criminals
And I can't make out your face
Amidst all the tears
Your eyeliner absorbs
Every ounce of my uneasiness
The pigs want me to finger you
But you're invisible

Your heart doesn't beat
So much as pound pavement cracks
Looking for the next lover
To ignore
In favour of the ones before
Your eyes search mine
For a convenient exit from the grotesquery
But this isn't about you and me
Not any more

We sit in the silences between words
We would lay in each other's arms
Were we necrophiles

Ah, those empty spaces
Those maddening silences
They have taken over the asylum
The mutes are inmates
And they're patiently mutating
Steadily evolving into doctors, nurses, liars
Exhausted, as am I
From the effort it took to jail us

The sun has eclipsed this
The house lights have gone down
I don't recognise you
In such darkness
You're a wishbone
To pry apart your pieces
Would be dumb unlucky, fuck
What can I do?
To unsex you

At your centre
(and I've been staring at it during the ad breaks)
Is a shipwreck
I've tried so hard
To unwreck it
But the storm sunk us both, darling
The difference is
I came up for air
You're still slurping particles
Of alchemical enmity
From the ocean bed
And you've been down there so long now
You're peeling barnacles
From your milkless breasts

The tasks you undertook
Are still five thousand leagues
Beneath the surface
There was no point waiting for you
You're happily unhappy down there
I'm free
An emotional terrorism survivor
A mental torment refugee

I've moved on to other waves
I am besotted with kinder women
Cutting shade on the distant horizon
Their silhouettes are becoming clearer
I can almost taste them
With the tongue I used to kiss you with
I will paint them with poetry
I shall fill their wounds with words
I will mend hearts instead of breaking them

I'm smiling, darling
Without you

And As the Silent Terror Grips Me

And as the silent terror grips me
I haunt the corridors of love
A nervous, nail-biting ghost
Swinging from wet, unfinished paintings,
Dry, sardonic poems, and golden chandeliers
Bright-eyed, beautiful lasses with tear jars
Filled with sorrow and sex and sympathy
Stare right through me
Reading the words scrawled on floral wallpapered walls
That I wrote in my own blood
Invisible poems, they are the only clue left
As to my whereabouts
A reminder that there is something
On the other side of the curtain that is sleep
My crooked mouth, my beady-eyed desire
My starlit drool and succulent, mouth-watering psychosis
My impossible embrace, transparent
To all but other dithering, anxious ghosts
Searching for a rare, precious heart
Looking for a way out of this dream
As if there is one

And as the silent terror grips me
I haunt the corridors of passion
A deranged spectre
A servant of delightful blood and blue flames
There is fire in my pen
I write my way into burning infernos
Inhaling acrid smoke and lungfuls of aberrant ash
I swill ink and silent whisky, I guzzle death

In this dream I hold the keys to the Asylum
I narrate the souls imprisoned here
I edit disease
I punctuate their scars
I tattoo escape routes onto fragile, crumbling minds
The Warden stares right through me
I am invisible to the Doctors, the expanding Shrinks
I long to kiss the pretty nurses
With my cracked black lips
The ink stains my throat and wells in my heart
Like forbidden molasses, sweet prophecy
There is poetry on my tongue
There are words in my eyes
All I can taste is chaotic literature and coma compassion
Sex, saliva, sweat and sadness
Statutes of liberty from anxiety and madness

And as the silent terror grips me
I haunt my cage
In this dream I cannot wake from
I stalk love itself
And love stares right back through me
Peering between the bars
Curious, looking for a lonely ghost
Unseeable, unknowable, unlovable
Even in death
Like inspired filth crimes
Of faith and abandonment
Like a tearful thought unthought
In an empty cage

You Are in a Movie Without Cameras

You can't believe your ears
For they have betrayed you
Voices only you can hear
Gather vociferous, spewing vulgarities
Into the empty rental space
Behind your eyes
There is a leaking tap in your mind
Drip, drip, drip it goes
Steadily filling the void that defines you

Naked perverts wearing raincoats
Chew on their cud, shooting glances your way
Shifty magicians, wizards of woe
Showering you with mind bullets

You are in a movie without cameras
The plot is writing itself
It is out of your control
The director is dead, murdered by paranoia
And waves of rapacious delusion
The crew split while the going was bad
Or perhaps they are invisible, like you
Perhaps you are only visible to yourself
And all the mirrors you pass
On your pathway to hellish stardom
Are in on the secret

No amount of medication can murder
The movie without cameras
Delusions of grandeur are seldom without suffering
But are they a reaction
To something buried deep down below?
Like the fact that we are insignificant

We mean so very little to so few
And we are running from time, spent
like death pennies, placed over our eyes
Blinded before death can take us
Robbed of true sight in a life
Not worth living

Lay down sweet conscience
You have been barricaded by the truth
Hold onto those you hold dear
For some, life and love are the same
A wrecking ball, a song of sorrow
A strange disease for the beautiful
With no cure

The Roadie and the Rock Star

And all they could think to say
Was goodbye
And that is all that you heard
An unquenchable ocean of sorrow
Spewing salty tears and froth
From sea to land
From a drowning grave to sun bleached sand
Right before your heart ceased to beat
Yet there are so many other words
That would do you justice
So many unexplored worlds
That would better describe this hurt

You were torn away from the mortal realm
Too soon
Maybe if we'd had more time?
Isn't that what we all want?
More time?
Before it all goes pear shaped
And our hearts are left twitching
Bleeding on the floor
I wish I could have loved you more
Let you know
While you were alive
But all I'm left with
Is this travesty of forfeiture and loneliness
For the world will never be the same
Without you
My flawed, sweet
Defeated friend

We shared a darkness that was profound
We were spectacular deviants
And it bound us together

The Roadie and the Rock Star
We both knew
Which one was you

I am left alone in a back alley
Reminiscing with your ghost
The spotlight illuminates an empty stage
I smile fondly through torrential tears
And share stories with your shadow
Who cannot hear me
Who cannot laugh or react in anger
Who cannot breathe like me
Who cannot see me here
Shaking like this

I still talk to you when I am alone
You never answer back

Part 2

The Church of Nothing

He went away for a while
It was necessary
He vanished from the swarthy skyline
Into a bottomless hole
A wingless angel
Blinded by the bleakest season
Before he rose again

I would yearn for his return
Ascendance requires insight
Wisdom necessitates great suffering
I would wait behind his eyes
I would clear a pathway to the skies
I would breathe when he would suffocate
So that one day
He might disappear amongst the stars

From my place perched upon his tongue
I tasted sickness
The narrator of sorrow foretold
Of a rapid descent into madness
Of a cure for ordinary happiness
Meant to sate the creeping fog that crept within
To forgive us now would be unforgivable
To forgive me is to forgive him

I watched from above
As he signed autographs for lunatics
In pay per view mental temples
A lord abortion in the countryside
A good times lobotomy
An exorcism for contrition
Free cocktails for private sector pricks
Olives skewered by murderous toothpicks
Dying a little more each day
In the shade of a T-shaped tree

He lived in the shadow of the Famous Mime
Until the Church of Nothing invited him in
Now he rescues kittens from volcanoes
He knows everything that God knows
In this prison, he is forgotten
In this laughing castle, he is king

No peace
No reason
The death train passing every station
No ceasing of such sorrow
No faith in some tomorrow
Nobody waiting for him on the other side
A curious sense of leaving life behind
Predicting his last decision
I watched him reach out from beyond the void
Beneath an avalanche of medication

I shadowed his every gesture
I watched from inside his mirror
Out to get him
Out to get me
He leapt from empty page to canvass rage
A blood portrait, drip
                drip
                    dripping

Transgressions and confessionals
Out to get him
Out to silence me
Over the screams of tortured animals
Over truth tellers, liars, blindest furies

The martyred mind of a dead astronaut
Cranium caved in
From the final blow that ended all his loneliness
A televisual testimonial
Broadcast live
Beamed directly to God's living room
Advertising sacrificial lambs' blood
To entertain the majority
And paint the righteous jury

He lived in the shadow of the Famous Mind
Until the Church of Nothing welcomed him in
Now he leaps skyscrapers in his underclothes
He knows everything that Jesus knows
In this Eden, he is sovereign
In this garden, he is king

I am the last poem he ever wrote
A prayer to the Church of Nothing
A cry for help to its congregation

I was the last gasp
Before his black heart ceased to beat

Gratitude

I found love
It was hiding in the guts of my pen
An ejaculation of ink
Was all it took to get my black heart beating
The arterial carousel had stopped turning
Now it's creeping in circles again
And, however brief,
I am just grateful for the ride

I found love
It was hiding in the eyes of a street urchin
In a back alley
Resting against a wall and gulping cheap wine
'Why can't you stop crying?' he asked
I shrugged my shoulders, sobbing
I handed him my empty wallet
And then fled
Running like hell, like shame,
Like unquenchable thirst
Deep into the unforgiving night

I found love
On a television gameshow
I had no answers
For questions that seemed designed
To beguile me
But the host had a gameshow grin
And a banal chutzpah
That I couldn't deny
Despite Denial being my specialty subject
I watched, transfixed
A passive consumer of mass psychosis

I found love
On a nondescript street corner
In the embers of a burning bin
The night was so cold
I thrust my hands deep into the fire
Gripped the only thing worth stealing
And wrenched out a brightly burning heart
I held it up to the light of the moon
My fingers on fire
And smiled

Like mine
It too was still beating
Hammering so hard
It blitzed out all reason
Gratitude
Like Love
Can be found in the most unexpected places

Minefield

Having a conversation with you
Is like tiptoeing through a minefield
I tread carefully
Lest I lose a limb

Repentagram

Misdeeds, paid for with death pennies
I am blinded by your trinkets
A half-masked man
Bound and gagged by love
Driven mad
In a serial killer's rental van

The past stalks me, drawing nearer
In every rear-view mirror
There is an unfolding sketch
Of a stick man
Staring up, in fear
At a descending noose
A man of letters
The game's end
Draws me closer

Repentagram
Metal as fuck
Fuck as metal
Excoriating screams
Beautiful, ripped-off faces
That you consider wearing
Over your own
Black bloody tongues, torn out
By cruel kisses
Bitten-off lips, tits, eye slits
That conceal glowing blue irises
Their pupils dilate as you masturbate

So, pull your teeth out
One by one by one
To correct your imperfections
Knowing all too well
That there is certain death in such perfection

(Drum solo)
(Drink Solo)
(Product placement sigh)

I'm sorry,
I won't do it again
And again
And again
And again

(Guitar solo)
(Drink Solo)
(Product placement groan)

Archipelago, Amigo, trombone solo

Consume death
And do it solo
The refreshingly effervescent slurp
The bewildered existentialist
The 'fuck it all' nihilist
The cheerful depression-ist
The resonant burp
Like a wildly swung claw hammer

Like a drunken exclamation mark
At the end of a predator's shit list
Read out loud to a slavering jury,
The morning after the crime

Repentagram
A diaphragm sent bent to Uranus
An under discovered planet
That only exists in free minds
Uterus Instagram,
A barely conceived blood clot plot
To take us all downtown

(and, note to reader)

Despite the chaos
The crippling anxiety
We are in a constant state of entropy
But we're having the time of our goddamn lives

Where we will find ourselves
In the morning
Is anyone's guess
But you can bet
I will truly regret
Being alive.

Mary Begs for an Abortion

There is something
Growing inside of me
Ever since God fucked me
One day it's heart
Will begin to beat
The time is creeping closer
Should I name it?
Embryo, simpatico
Infanticide, insanity
Foetus, defeat us
Righteous murderer
of my body, of my mind
My sanctuary ripped apart,
dis-sanctity

For Christ's sake, God
I am pregnant with your child
And I am only fourteen

What is this lump inside of me?
Clinging on, pulsing as it grows
Homunculus, parasite of dis-vision
Harvester of the book of sorrows
A view from my womb
Soon to be tomb
The gravestones stretch out on the horizon
Willing life to go on
As I suffer

Expel the stench of life in me
Growing, suckling
This symbiont, a holy pig in uterus mud,
Squealing for a divine mother
To feed it, mourn it before it's time
Gnawing on an umbilical noose
A sacred criminal, unchosen
Defiant, filling me up
A flyblown meat miracle

Hold my heart, my shaking hands
And kill it
Tear it out
Before its divine mind takes shape
Quickly, before it learns to speak
Speedily, Masters, before it begins to pray
For those that gather in worship
Will surely send it,
like all good soldiers,
To the War
To a predetermined suicide
On the front lines
For they are everywhere

Dispense of the saint
The tiny monster growing inside of me
Have a kind heart
Lend a bloody, red right hand
So that we might tear it out together
And be ridden
Of this cancellation cancer

God, get your filthy hands off me!

(Stroke, smack, lick, suck, fuck, crack…)

God, get your holy prick away from me!

Kill the well-meaning child
Before he lives to die

Murder the potential
Of the spiritual martyr
Empty my womb
Scrape the walls clean

For Christ's sake, God
You perverted fiend
I am pregnant with your child
And I am only fourteen

I offer my womb to the angels
A holy temple
To be torn asunder
So that I might be set free

Requiem Cliché

1.

And when I die
Only then
Will people listen
And when I pass
Only then
Will people understand
What I was trying to say
For alive
I am an unloved god
In death
I will live forever

2.

In truth
Death rarely guarantees immortality
Usually, an artist
And their life's work
Is forgotten
Discarded
Much like their corpse
Those who survive
This brutal transition
Are either lucky
Or truly, transcendently unique
Yet by the time acceptance
And recognition arrives
These saints of creative genius
Are too dead
To give a fuck

3.

We dream of glory in death
We, the arbiters of imagination
We dream of the glory and accolades
That never came our way
In life
Is that sad?
Or is it simply the plight
Of the uncelebrated artist
Some of us long to die
Just to be finally understood
Some of us lust for death
So that the party
The awards ceremony
The weeping funeral
Might follow us into the afterlife
Where we can finally smile
And weep in self congratulations
Where we are finally understood
And appreciated
When it is obviously
And patently
Far too fucking late

Punched in the Face by Gandhi

I saw it all before it happened
I followed my decapitated head
Into an alleyway
And hid there…

I have been hiding for millennia

Punched in the face by Gandhi
Like a misplaced sense of irony
I wanna go the full twelve rounds
With a pacifist
Instead, I'm foaming at the mouth
Dreaming of kissing strange women
Feigning death
In Dali-esque prison landscapes
My reputation
Traded in for Tupperware sexuality

How can you leave me?
You've never even met me
Lips, tits, hips, slits
Succulent, barbecue saucy
Sweat, saliva, cum and men of the sea
Death by sexy
Eyes that mirror the bluest sky
Eyes that paint me into exquisite gutters,
Corners, black gardens, flying sources
That exacerbate my wrongness,
My strongness, my nightshade eclipse
My nothingness
On any other planet
I would still ache for you

In my dreams
You are attempting to wake me
In vain
In my dreams
We fuck like saints
We're inked with regrettable tattoos
We're pretty
Just like Jesus made us to be

The silent, the violent
The righteous servant
Serving us up
To the beautiful people

I like the way you talk
Like everyone is listening
I like the way you walk
Like everyone is watching
I'll take you out on the town
I'm loaded
My swear jar is overflowing with fucks

I want to sit in on the Jury
Debating right behind your eyes
Deciding whether to free you before you're ready
So that we can get on with
Dancing, kissing, pissing, suffering

All I can describe
Is the corner I'm painted into
Limiting my unlimited reality

I want to eat your tongue like an aphrodisiac,
Lick your hairy eyeballs,
Suck your salacious kiss,
Infiltrate your impenetrable mind
But my pallbearers have abandoned
The coffin I was writing in
They fled my deathbed
Right when it was time for us to snuggle
This funeral is now a bloody shambles
The Devil has possessed my pen
And there isn't a practising exorcist for miles

I can't see a damn thing inside this box
I can't kiss you
I can't lick you
I can't fuck you
I can't hold you in my arms
And dream of zero

But I can write you
Into the ink-stained pages of eternity
And, thanks to me
You will be this way forever

Nonsense, said the Drunk

The Reality Surgeon cut deep into the cadaver
Severing its pulp gullet
With a literary scalpel
The audience gasped and shimmied
Writhing about on the surrounding floor
Like bemused fish, suffocating on stolen air

The knitting circle drew closer
Furiously threading and weaving
Through the void left by yesterdays in crowd
Several examples of misanthropic wonderment
Analysed the scene and then rejected it
As if on principle alone
As if there was nothing to be learnt
From such scurrilous debauchery

The King bawled like an abandoned child
The Queen snickered, nervously
Wringing her hands at the expense
Of her overly emotional husband
Yet revelling in his pain nonetheless
None of this would matter
Were it not for the plight of the slaves
Who promptly erupted
Like a family of wounded volcanos
Their molten insides
Spilling across the floorboards
Burning holes in the stage and murdering
All the actors with scalding lava

And Death
Like a nonsensical Mime
Silently buggered the Reality Surgeon
And everyone left the theatre
Happily unhappy
Their petty lives forever altered
And their night out on the town
Ruined by a most startling display
Of preposterous horror

None of it made any sense
So, they burnt down the theatre
Killing those that had stayed behind
To dutifully clean up the mess
They requested refunds for their tickets
And then caught buses like diseases
Travelling home, sick
Puking into brown paper bags
Praying to a dubious version of God
That this was the end of all endings
And no one would ever have to go through it
Ever again

Le Petite Mort (ification)

The end of the conversation
The numb explosion
The feeling of regret
One gets
When the phone line suddenly goes dead

The climax in the debate
When we realise, we're both wrong
And no one is going to win the argument

The detonation of stillness
The systematic extermination of madness
And the cockroaches who have over run your mind
And taken over the asylum

The feeling of guilt
After you've blown it all
The crescendo in the orchestral wall
Swelling, then breaking like a wave
The crescendo that leaves you spent
Rather than elated
The crescendo that leaves you alone
With your thoughts
When you'd much prefer to be accompanied
By thoughtlessness
And unthinking friends

The distaste you feel
After your final death row meal
Then the pep in your step
As you skip
Fancy free
To your scheduled execution

A Church Without Windows

I live in a church without windows
Something in me is broken
There are no sunrises or sunsets here
No psychedelic horizons
No panoramic views
No murderers but yours untruly
On the six o'clock news
There are broken Christmas lights in my eyes
Life, lingers like leprosy, in my loins
I am a prostitute selling words
For a petulant pimp
My body belongs to the Lord

Suffering is for pigs
Bred for their meat, fattened for RSL buffets
Pasta and prayer, crackling for cracking
As all minds do, under this insufferable regime
Eventually

Do you think like I do?
Do you love like I do?
If not, I'm afraid you're destined for the abattoir
As all well-meaning swine are
Living to die and be devoured
Branded hero, undeserving coward
Your skull is fuckable
Like a hollowed-out vagina
Sweating from the stress of loving you
Moist from playing the hero, the dismayed maiden

Piggy, piggy, pig
Smut, slut, shamer, shaman, conjuror
Dressed to the knives like a saint
All seeing
So, you might unsheathe your sharpened blade
And pluck out his eyes

Drink the ooze from my lungs
It's black and tarred with regrets
So, get busy dying
And cease your ceaseless trying
Death is only inevitable
For those who lived in the first place
For everyone else
It's a futile display of feigned intention

I live in a church without windows
I pray to a God who despises me
In the darkness that I call
home

Part 3

The Exorcism was a Thundering Success

1.

These words fear themselves
It's as if the ink were attempting to hide beneath the paper
Sinking deeper in plain sight

Lord, give me the courage to be less than
Lord, give me the strength to accept that you are not there for me
Lord, there is no laughter to carry me above the waves

I have been gone for eons, in my time
As mere months ticked by in your world
As I shuddered and hid from the Monster
I have folded in on myself
My wit and guile stole away on a death ferry
To the other side
They never made it to the opposing shore

2.

The waiting party were few
Embracing a far slighter man than they had known
They passed their decree,
In tones both wistful and melancholy,
They spoke:

'The light is gone from his eyes
His shadow casts no shape
It has no form nor character
The grandeur must have fled the tomb
Of this yawning spectre
Right before he leapt into the boneyard
And denounced the departure of his spirit.'

'For he creeps upon the sand and leaves no footprints
Everything about the creature is banal, featureless
An ordinary sculpture, carved by ordinary hands
There is nothing remarkable here
No spark
No chaotic chuckle
No signs of an imagination
That was once noteworthy
The winds whistle between his ears
As if there were no mind
No visceral cerebrum to catch and distort them
Into something worth being, worth knowing
Worth reading or listening to.'

'No, there is little to no life left here
None that we can see
If there were once colourful thoughts
If there was once a dark light trapped in these eyes
It has long since perished
Or worse, been forcibly removed.'

'How does the creature stand?
For once a monster cowered beneath this cowl
Now all that remains is a dull ache of a man
Devoid of merriment and laughter
Empty of thoughts except those that paint him as other
As deficient as he was once aberrant
A tearful yawn in the place of something that was abhorrent
To all but those who knew him
For what could be worse?
Is this all that is left of a man?
Once the demon has been cast out?'

They all agreed
It had been a most disappointing return
For Miracles become Monsters become Nothings
And all that was left that they could fathom
Standing in the wretched grave of the Monster
That they once called a friend
Was an ordinary ghost

A Lonely Old Man

Sometimes I pray
To an all-loving void
Yet then I regret it
Like I've done something wrong
Something that cannot be taken back
No matter how many
Hail Marys or Our Fathers
I bellow into the emptiness, silently
Even though in my head
I'm screaming
Like a banshee, like an abandoned babe

Gimme breast milk,
But make it a double, a triple, a tiple
Whisky is clearer, misty-eyed,
Like a polluted conscience
I am being stalked by succulent nipples
Gimme free to air TV, gimme HIV
I wanna party with the lepers
I wanna be a one-man band, starring on MTV
I wanna fuck the world
And be loved for it
Gimme Covid, gimme PTSD

I have given up on getting your attention
One of us is stupid
I'm the other guy

Somewhere in the world
In a one-bedroom flat
Most probably drunk on social media
There is an old man masturbating to my words
He has no family or friends, no prospects
He is dying of loneliness and probably cancer
God bless him

An Unattended Funeral

The biggest and most profound
Display of love
That anyone gets to experience
In and out of their lifetime
Is when they are truly dead

Think about that for a moment
And revel in your shame
How dare you take a human being
Who meant so much when their heart was beating
And reduce them to a death valentine

It's easier for you
When they can't reply
It's more convenient for you
When they can't kiss
Or hug you back
When all is said and done
Humans are selfish denialists
We like to believe
They have gone somewhere else
Where they can look down upon us
Mourning them
Where they can appreciate their own funeral
Where they realise they were loved
And they can't reply

The truth is
They can't
And for the most part
Despite deserving every eulogy and tear
They just left us
Mostly unloved
With their flaws the focus
Of our nebulous conceit

Wake up
And love your friends
Your wives
Your husbands
Your children
While they are still breathing

Death truly is a tragedy
Love, unexpressed, is our problem
Funerals are a waste of everyone's time

I love you.

Creeping Jesus

Creeping Jesus
Shoplifting blues, stealing used Bibles
It's the five-finger discount sale
Tattered and torn and reborn
In Christ's image, thieving
From an Op Shop extravaganza
Then tearing out the pages
And engulfing them
Choking on Revelations
Blowing Matthew, Mark, Luke and John
Swallowing scripture with a gag reflex
One parable at a time
Consuming God

Creeping Jesus
Pissing himself on the bus
And smiling
From Buranda to the Cultural Centre

Creeping Jesus
Camping out in the Garden of Eden
On a park bench
With a towel for a blanket
Sharing his holy blood with devoted mosquitos
Homeless and halfway happy
Picking apples from an abandoned tree
Years since he showered
Eternity waits for him to bathe in its mystery
Shits himself on the street corner
Where he begs for durries and loose change

Creeping Jesus
His father died in the bottom of a bottle
A pitiful fatality,
He drowned in his own whisky
His Mother has Alzheimer's
She's unhappily in a home
Doesn't recognise her son
Can't recall his name
She used to belt him around the head with a Bible
Licked his pasty buttocks with a leather strap
Welts and scars and blood and truth
Mental and physical
Faith beaten into youth

Creeping Jesus
Mother caught her son when he was only ten
In the boudoir
Sniffing panties and bras
Mother taught her son
One of many lessons then
Welts and scars
Welts and scars
Too late to tame the serpent
Too late to spare the god
And spoil the child

Creeping Jesus
Cask wine, Merlot, dry red
Like the true Messiah was a drunkard
Like being left for dead
Hitch hiking his way to the CBD,
stinking of heaven
With a pension card and a crucifix lanyard
Bumming smokes outside the 7 Eleven

Hot dog fragments in his beard
Tomato sauce like sacrificial blood
Staining his ratty flanny
Shakespearian, painted tragic
Macbeth's guilt, the mad King of Lear
Just a few more bucks till the Off Licence
Is a certainty
Reeking of sin, untamed chaos and stale beer
Piss, pandemonium and magic

Creeping Jesus
Superstar in the city of lies
King of bums in the Fortitude Valley
Dishevelled long grey hair
Jesus' tangled beard
Microchips in his teeth
Messages from the supermarket intercom
Government surveillance
If only they knew
The six o'clock news
Always telling him what to do

Creeping Jesus
He pays no mind
Can't afford it
Searching for a cross in the suburbs
One that might nail his uncertainty
To a Christmas city tree
There is always a park bench
To sleep away his days
He will always be
A maligned deity

There is a strange comfort
To be found
In not having a home
There is hell in every government handout
Like another discarded webster pack
Asylum beds and psychiatric meds
Just dreams untold, stories unfolding
Cos no one will listen
And there is no one to talk to

Creeping Jesus
Divinity or insanity?
It's entirely up to a God
Who gave up years ago
Is this freedom?

You decide.

Smiley Face

Smiley Face works at the abattoir
Killing cows with kindness
He slurps meat shakes through a cardboard straw
And labels his lunch with a sweaty heart
Devoured like a vote of no conscience

He trawls Facebook in the small hours
Instagram is for narcissists
Twitter is for bores
Porn is just confusing now days
He mows the lawn with someone else's Wifi
Cleans his laptop screen with brown vinegar
Clears his browser history with a handshake
Dreams of giving to charity
Such dreams will keep him poor

Smiley Face has two thousand friends
Spends the nights alone
Photographs of sunsets make him angry
Landscapes make him cry
Every Like is a hand grenade recurring
A pulled pin for an unspun pun
A cavalcade of restless emojis
To fill the emptiness within

And somewhere in the darkness
Smiley Face watches kittens frolicking in a video
He laughs out loud at memes mocking the war
He drags Russian tanks with Ukrainian tractors
Wakes just in time to bus it to the abattoir

A Like to fuel his morning coffee
A Like to end all Likeability
An unspent nuke deserving of a smiley face
Climate change and road rage
All Liked on someone else's page
Photographs of angry sunsets stretching out forever
As if in some hall of in-turned circus mirrors
Cares clicked
Turn to crying eyes and LOLs and death tolls
And decapitated puppies
And mountains of dead bodies
And odes to dead celebrities
And the real cost of war
And a drowning Covid case
Swept away by another flood
Followed by a rash of bushfires and soaring temperatures
Burnt down houses and homeless kittens
Who left the litter
Just when they couldn't get any cuter
Hitchhiking their way to Hollywood
On their way to something better

After work
Smiley Face kicks off his shoes
Logs on to Facebook
Wonders whether to cry
Be angry
Whether to care
He practises his smile in a laptop mirror
That reflects everything and understands nothing
'WOW' he thinks.

Until Smiley Face can think of something better
A well-placed heart will have to do

Sunday

The carcass of a dead church
Washes up on the night shore
Its blue-tinged, discoloured skin
Catches the light of the moon
Like a waterlogged star
Ripples in the water from whence it came
Hint at further betrayal

I sit down in the sand
By its side
And delicately stroke its lifeless face
I lean in
And whisper something
Like
Die, you fucker
Or
I miss you
Then I stand like it doesn't matter
Shake off the sand
Smile sadly
And walk away

An Illuminated Light Bulb

How many psychologists
Does it take
To change a light bulb?
None.
None of them are qualified
No one wants to change
Not really
We're all just faking it
Saving our erections
Till someone sexier comes along

I would just like to take a moment
To thank my sponsors
For the win:
Lethargy, anarchy, alcohol, denial
Inspiration never sponsored me
But I'd like to thank her anyway
She's my irresponsible pal, my gal
And she's never let me down

You think you know everything
I'm not seeking your help
Just relief from reality
You think it's lonely at the top?
How does it feel at the bottom?
That's where I reside

I'd donate blood
If I didn't need it so badly
No, I'm not a donor
Nor a reality doctor
I'm a literary loner
In urgent need of a shallow editor
And some confidence medication
Perhaps even a fistful of personality pills
Would suffice

This room is getting smaller
And I'm expanding
Pretty soon I'll be pressed against the walls
Breathing will become more difficult
My heart, pumping ink
Will cease to beat
And I will cease to write

You think you know everything
But you don't know me
Drinking myself to death
In the shadow of a T-shaped tree

I'd just like to remind you
To brush your teeth, floss vigorously
To bathe regularly, wash your balls
And above all, read my writing

All the instructions mentioned above
Will increase the quality of your life
And sustain you

Either that
Or the fates are truly against us
And as per usual
I have wasted my precious fucking time

You think you know everything
Have you ever wondered what it would be like
To know less than you think you do
Either way, it was a pleasure to talk AT you
Without the unusual interruptions
That go along
With being your friend

The Fear

The fear
Keeping me locked away
The fear
Negating freedom
The fear
Fencing off all entrances and exits
No way out or in
Mind crimes and dysphoria
Despair, depression
Disconnection
Gnawing on the hand that feeds
Psychological cannibalism
Eating away at my mind, my heart
Feasting on
The fear
Dining at a restaurant for psychopaths
A buffet for the emotionally disturbed
Cracked
Like a disagreeable egg
Broken
Like snapped vertebrae
A cheerful serpent, fangs fixed
To the throat of the King
Of fear

A Hopeless Romantic Reading Poetry to the Dead

Physical disintegration is unkind
To even the handsomest sailor
Pretty much every woman alive
Is now out of my league
Hell, most corpses would pass me over
But at least they listen
Some are patient and enjoy my word abominations
So, if you're looking for me
I'll be at the local morgue
Reading romantic poetry
To pretty cadavers

Bad Actor

Memento Mori
'Remember that you must die'
So, let's make the least of this
Shall we?

Mind pollution
Body pollution
Eradication of the temple
The obliteration of beauty
The art of rotting
Is a shallow procession
Of gluttonous self-kissing
And my mirror needs cleaning

You never understood me
You never tried
Now I hide in plain sight
A reverse miracle
I would rather be obscured by dark clouds,
than held up to the light

I am a fiction
A bad actor
This page is my stage

Your scrutiny defames me
My eyes turn inwards
Rolling back into my skull
Peering at the wall I built
To cage a terrified mind
Marvelling at the handiwork it took
To fence myself in
And keep you out

I am an ashtray
Stub your cigarettes out in my eyes
I am an ember in December
Floating on hot Christmas breath
I am human debris
A wreckage in poetic motion

I would rather die on my feet,
than live on my knees
But my legs are gelatine, sky pilot jelly
And it would take more,
than your fervent misconceptions
To unravel me

Every poem is a violent fiction
I am a leprous thespian
Selling off my unreal estate
Limb by limbless whim
I am a fanciful conception of someone
That you don't know and never will
Every 'I' is a lie
A discourse aflame for pyromantics
A toe dipped into a symbolic order
Where devils are born

I am a bad actor
This page is my stage
I piss smoke and shit mirrors
And I do it all for you

Part 4

Cheers

The mornings are the worst
My body and mind
Deprived of liquor
Proceed to rattle and shake
The nausea, the coughing, the desire to puke
They are violent in nature

I am indebted to the Kings and Queens
Of royal addiction
Yet there is no glory in this hole
I am incarcerated
By my own urges

There is no grand plan
Just the whims of addiction
I don't wish to die
Not yet
Maladjusted and mutating
The disease is taking over
My thirst is getting more extreme

I would get down on my knees and pray
But there is no God
No Messiah in the bottom of this bottle
Just a trap door
Leading to the next fix
I wish the urge could be supplanted
By a self-love
I have no right to call my own

I broke this heart
Myself
There is no replacement
And no fix for it
I'm guzzling shadows
The room is getting darker
With every swallow
Yesterday is a pale imitation
Of a black tomorrow

Tequila Mockingbird

Time wounds all heels
It's like stepping on a clock
And regretting it
All I can think of
And this rules my thoughts
Is that I've ruined everything
I took ten steps forwards
Then eleven steps backwards
Progress is in reverse
Like a car
Backing over a twitching corpse
And the corpse is my own
Except it's drunk and bloated
Alcohol is my enemy
Alcohol is my best friend
We spend a lot of bad quality time together

Don't Kill Yourself, Just Kiss Me

I don't want to leave you
Out in the streets amongst the creeping urchins
And crumbling, concrete wildflowers
I want to take you into my home
Clothe you in caffeine
Brew you
Like a pot
Of existential coffee

I don't want to leave you
Hanging from a noose
Dangling from the branch
Of an exotic tree
I'd much rather invite you
To drink with me
In the gutter
We could compare
Our favourite stars
We could deconstruct
Our chosen constellations
Then deflower each other's minds

You Are Necessary

Reality is belief
Truth is not popular consensus
Question everything you think you know
The answers are never
As obvious as they appear
But don't give up hope
And don't give in
Which side of the fence you are on
Is less important
Than who built the damn fence
Who thought of it
In the first place

We're universally divided
Faith is divisive
God may not exist
But faith in him certainly does
He's manifest in so many minds
In so many religions
That reality has become redundant
There is kindness in my heart
If there is a heaven
And despite everything
I somehow ended up there
I would be bored shitless
The tedium of self-righteous saints
Beckons the unbeliever

Love can bring us together
But it tears so many apart
When it fails
Love is not perfect
And neither am I

Perhaps we need these schisms
It's easier to fight with others
Than it is to fight yourself
Conquering your own ego
Should be a noble pursuit
But chaos is just so delicious
I want to devour the madness
I want to feast on personal anarchy
The war is inside of me
But it is reflected in the eyes of strangers
Who strut like stalkers
Who spread cancers
Like mass media murderers
Who rape me of certainty
And cause me to question my heart

I believe we should break bread
With our neighbours
No matter what they believe
But I am in hiding
Part of a witness deconstruction program
That keeps me locked away
Besides, I have grown fond of the darkness
And there is only so much love
I have to give

Death, rip me apart
You are necessary

Unlucky Stars

Count your lucky stars
Deconstruct
Your personal constellations
Patterns of sparkling angels
In the skies
Could be suns beamed to us
Billions of years too late
Dead beacons of hope
That we can no longer rely on
To save us from ourselves

I have a Guardian Angel
(My Mum says so, and she'd know)
Yet she sunk her teeth into my neck
When I let her down
For the thousandth time
Guardian angels are curious creatures
Seraphim, on Adderall and Morphine
To numb them from the responsibility
Of their roles

Now there's no one to protect me
From the charismatic jackals
That stalk the wastelands
Looking for unweaned babes to feast on
And I am rapidly losing blood

Drink up! Drink up!
For the time of miracles has passed
And the age of false prophets
Of malevolent saints and deranged soothsayers
Is upon us

Believe what you want
I don't believe a word

Deathstination

Murdered by emojis
Upstaged by neurotic ninja stars
I boarded the last train
Deathstination Shangri-La
I was leaving everything behind
It would be difficult
Starting over
In the afterlife
I knew that
Still, I had to try

***

I rued the day I lived
So, I got on with dying
I schooled myself in the dark arts
Purchased a rhyming Bible
I tore pages from my pulp heart
As if they were unknowable, unreadable
I tore out the spine of a love dictionary
To ensure it would never define love again
I burnt my personal diary
and roared
Like a bedwetting God
Outwitting a rabid guide dog
For blind people with anger issues
and snored
Like a Brontosaurus
Quoting an ancient sex Thesaurus
And humping synonyms

and so, I died
Clenching anal rosary beads
Dreaming of where it all went wrong
For me
Knowing all too well
That Gehenna was for overachievers
Motivational life coaches
and educated cockroaches
For anyone who's anyone
Heaven was the place to be

Perhaps
I had fucked too many Crystal Dolphins
and it had all gone to my head?
Perhaps
The man upstairs
Would turn me away?
and I'd trash the pearly gates
In a void rage
Bereft of purpose
With no place left to call a home

No angels to massage my aching shoulders
No Sisyphus to push the boulders
No earthen realm to claim me
No Bottle-os nearby
No gutter to get drunk in
No movie stars twinkling in the sky
No way to get back in
To the seedy bar that turfed me out

A life of undead homelessness
On the cruel streets
Outside the inside
Of an exclusive
Members only afterlife club

***

Mourned by crying emojis
Watched closely
by a gallery of lazy I's
I boarded the last train
Deathstination Shangri-La
Armed with a pen, an arrogant amen,
and a guide to tantric masturbation
Dead and broken and dreaming
I smiled sadly
As I left the station
I waved goodbye to the world
On my way
To the great Gigabyte in the sky

The Medication Vending Machines Are Empty

Grandiose delusions are a reaction to insignificance
Infamy is a burning bitch branch
A drowning witch
On a fucked-up family tree
It would take a thousand misplaced commas
And a full stop dot apostrophe
To edit this literary gob
And punch the teeth from my grin
It would take a rhyming bible
A well punctuated smile
Marked by exclamations and semi erect colons
To subdue the crime that is guilty poetry

Punch the keys
Until they're unconscious
Headbutt the screen
Till you bleed and the window is cracked and broken
Reach for the horizon
Beyond the monitor
And pull back a bloody stump
I dream of unfucking your life
But your delusional mind is elsewhere
I dreamt a dream of you smiling
Then I woke, and found myself
In the meddlesomeness of nowhere

I want to take the pain of your nature
Away from you
But there's no cure for your insanity
The medication vending machines are empty
They're out of pills
They're thrilled
They're killed
To watch you twitch, shake, dither in your loneliness
And slowly stumble away

This parade of romantic suitors
Is a façade
You're a frail, fragile creation
Of your own design
Rotting for the cameras that aren't there
You're a sweet, embittered egotist
But the worst of us
Love you nonetheless

The Last Resort

I was smoking crack with Jesus
and he said the damnedest thing,
'I didn't mean to save you
Or anyone
I just wanted to die.'

I gasped inwardly
and then goofily smiled
I was just fucked up enough
To believe this guy

The monkey on Jesus's back screeched
Like it wanted something
All mad hunger, bug eyed, brown fur,
with a tail like a severed whip
Jesus handed it the crack pipe
and it took a greedy hit
I have never seen Jesus without his monkey

When the monkey was done
Jesus handed me the pipe
It was my turn

The Narrator of Sorrows said,

'Suicide is a popular Last Resort
Located on a tropical island
Surrounded by a beautiful coral reef
And several hundred man eating sharks
There is no way off the island
(Or off the expensive Last Resort
that sits on its rim like a wart on a cancerous,
albeit luxurious, sphincter)
Other than dead'

'Patrons either enjoy the watered-down cocktails,'
The Narrator continued,
'The plump, delicious shrimp
The rigged casino,
The bounteous buffets,
The warm piss-filled spas,
The cancerette sections for smokers,
The Keno, the Blow,
The tattooed waitresses with the scars,
The wacky tobacky tokers,
The LSD urinal cakes in the latrines,
The unbeatable (but very companionable) pokie machines
Or. They. Choose. Death'

'The ultimate way out
The holiday of holidays
Eternal slumber
And bad blood in the holy water'

'Shut the fuck up!' said Jesus testily
Silencing the Narrator of Sorrows
Losing his well cultivated cool

He handed me the crack pipe
(Grinning like a leprous loon,
squinting through glazed red peepers)
and removed the monkey from his back,
Throwing the animal onto the sand
'Time for a swim, Basil,' he said
His voice dripping with mischief and grand import

Jesus stood up
Stripped off his robes
and then enthusiastically high fived me
'See ya round, Sport,' he said

He then proceeded to run,
Butt naked with his monkey in hot pursuit
Down the beach and into the water,
cackling, hooting and hollering
Blabbering into the sky

It was if someone was watching him,
Or listening, I thought
From all the way up there

There were violent splashes
Explosions of froth
As several fins closed in
(Jesus's monkey paced the water's ebbing edge
Too afraid to enter)
The surface of the ocean went dark red
Spreading out into a gorgeous, petalesque plume
Jesus's head and then halo disappeared
In quick succession
To the sound of a final, resonant burp

Then there was a gurgle and a pop
As if a plug had been dislodged
From a porcelain sink overflowing with blood
The salty vermillion sea receded
The murderous sharks and the echoes of hundreds
Of entertaining but mindless parables
Swirled ever downwards, sucked out of existence
Slurped into the slavering gob of the hole
That had opened up
In the guts of the earth itself

I took a long inconsiderate drag on the crack pipe
The monkey scurried up the beach
and sat down beside me
Clearly distressed but defeated

'Will we ever see that crazy bastard again?'
I asked the monkey, incredulously
'Oh, he'll be back,' Basil replied knowingly,
absently scratching at his flea-sullied fur
'He pulls this sort of shit all the time.'
'Yeah, I guess he has no choice,' I replied ominously
And at that,
I generously passed the crack pipe to my new friend

'Anyone would think he had a death wish,'
said the Narrator of Sorrows,
his words curling in on themselves
Like poisoned leeches
Retreating from succulent host skin
Like unforgivable sin
and the fatal, fiery glory
Of celebrity automobile crashes

After that, neither of us said a word
We couldn't think of a damn thing
The monkey and I
There was nothing left to say

We looked up into the drug addled sky
We smiled grimly, knowingly, fearfully
Reeling from deep wet kisses of mad crack
and then mock solemnly,
Like we knew something that Jesus didn't

We both nodded our heads in agreement
'Amen,' we chanted in unison,
'A-Fucking-Men.'

Im(mortality)

All my questions
Have been met with silence
Still, it's just another scream
Muted, by the remote control
Muted, by the plastic bag over my head
Entropy is absolutism
There is an alarming clock in my head
Each ticktock is a heartbeat
A fist in the face
That I will never know again
Life itself is running out on me

The relationship between poem and poet
Is masturbation
There's no truth to either
But like any effective illusion
They need each other
Words negate
Words empower
If only I knew where to put them
Where they fit best
Alongside each other

The screen goes blank
I open my eyes
I'm staggering through a forest
Nooses hang from every tree
A car pulls up
A window is wound down
A stranger, with bullet holes for eyes
Asks me for directions
But not even I know where I am
I can't help you, I say
He leaps out of the car
And rapes me
I laugh through the whole sordid ordeal

Dreams turn to nightmares
As they often do
Every time I open my eyes,
I awaken somewhere else

Drink up, drink up
Let's raise a toast to yesterday
I have travelled too far
To go back
Yet here I am
With a drink in one hand
To stave off the shaking
And my dick in the other
Heaven was designed for heathens
Just like me

Rolling dice, bones, stones
Celebrating death
As if it were just another birthday
Blow out the candles
And pray for someone to turn on the lights
Bury my face in cake
Headbutt the desert with a celebratory thud
Sponge, cream and jam
Fills my nostrils, eyes and gob

Scuttle around on the floor
Like a bewildered cockroach
Searching in vain for match sticks
So that the lights in my eyes
Might return, and dance
For the invisible audience
Singing
'Here we are now, drain us'
I discovered a soul
In the bottom of a bottle
It may as well be mine

The inverted cross
I carved into my forehead
Is just a pretzel
Satanism bores me
The devil feels the same way

All my songs are out of tune
All my words are broken
I am a true disbeliever
Is there peace to be found
Among all the missing pieces?
My heartbeat is fading
Put your ear to my chest, darling
And just listen
In this cornucopia of illusions
The processes of living and dying
Are one and the same

Your Ghost

Your ghost lingers
It fingers
My eyes and my mouth
Filling every orifice
A physical apparition, never departing
Yet never staying long enough
That I can get a fix on its intentions
Your ghost haunted me as a child
It smothered my dreams, in fear
I fled my bed, my silhouette, my shadow
I wept in the corner, and shook

Now I am a man, still frightened, still shaking
Like that impressionable child
Still absorbed by darkness
And what those dark corners withheld
How do I reconcile death?
When it is stalking me
Are you Jesus, God, the Holy Spirit
Or are you a serpent
Sent to poison me, to pollute my mind
And steal away my sanity

I hide in the most obvious places
It's laughable
It is a miracle you have not found me, by now
I call out to you, ghost
I beckon you to reveal yourself
To reveal me to the minions
Who follow you like slaves
Like leeches on a Messiah's skin
Feeding on faith, on holiness and disbelief
On blood as wine, as whisky, like swine

Your ghost
Were you once a man?
A god, a deity, a dog?
Or have you always been this way?
I can't decide whether to loathe you or love you
Yet you follow me around
Cornering my every thought
Like I did you a disservice
In a former life
Like you live to haunt me
And without that
You have no other reason to exist

Your ghost
Whether you are holy, or just a graveyard pest
I have no other recourse
Than to mock you
For I fear, otherwise
You will never leave me alone
And I will be forced to kill us both

Part 5

Knickers

Clever enough to know better
Dumb enough to do it all over again
We are the sum of our mistakes
We are elaborate portraits of our flaws
Masterpieces of peccadillo and slathered oil

The black sun is throbbing
Like a cancerous heart suspended in the sky
The moon is made of rancid meat
I want to take a bite out of it
Midnight food poisoning and light
Reflected in crimson oceans
And dying to cry eyes, lusting
To lick and lap at the tears
Of mad, lascivious women
Weeping in soul cages
And madder than stabbed snake men

Would you have me lie to you?
Just so you might like me.
Would you have me sell myself
To the lowest bidder
Just so I might commit my heart
To your venom
And the throes of emotional slavery?

Repelled by human chattel
Possessed by a loveable demon
Stalked by fetid blue cheese and death crackers
I'm knackered
Blacked out and bruised by your irascible gaze
If you keep looking at me
This way
I may have to find somewhere dangerous
To hide away
And await the return of my courage

Can I perchance borrow your knickers?
I will return them when I am finished living
I will return them unsoiled and smelling of flowers
And the perfume of an unloved God's loins
If you get them back
It will be as if I had not lived at all

Can I perchance borrow your knickers?
I will return them to you when I am wise, decrepit and old
I will return them to you when I am no longer heartbroken
I will return them to you when I have given up on love

You will never get them back

The Eroticisation of a Hyper Reality TV Food Disorder

The cooking show is a strange disease
Catch it while you can
Watch it as it's spreading
It's on every channel
On every scrumptious satellite dish
A time of the signs, a belly reckoning
A bad taste sensation
There's nothing much else worth watching

And yet…
We can't smell the food
We can't taste the food
Can we?
We are merely voyeurs
Salivating among millions
Of hungry viewers

Pornography isn't sex
Cooking shows are not about food
Yet your pants are down to your ankles
The remotest control marinating in one hand
Basted genitals cradled in the other
You're hungry for something
That doesn't exist
And the whole damn family is watching

It's a culinary competition
We watch people cook the food
We watch people smell the food
We watch people taste the food
We observe celebrities eating something
That is unknowable
Unquantifiable
We watch them chew it
We watch them swallow it
If we could
We'd watch them digest it
For there are thousands of angles
And there are hundreds of cameras
But none reside in their mouths, throats,
Bellies or bowels

If only we could taste the TV
If only we could smell the TV

Consumers of the mass media kitchen
Passive, informed by sights n' sounds
Dull fuckings and duck dumplings
The gnash, the snarl and the swell
Spices, devices and celebrity judges
Ten minutes to go till the bell

Actors concoct the illusion
Editors up the drama
Gimme Smellavision!
Gimme Tastetestavision!
Hooray for high crime cuisine
Food is in fashion
Consume the ubiquitous façade

Through the TV eye
The chocolate in that cake
May as well be faeces
There's no way to know for sure
Either way
The shit on display
Is goddamn delicious

At least you can't get fat
From watching *MasterChef*

Gehenna

I am a parade of warbling, sobbing tears
A factory of fear
And unquenchable despair
Anxiety rules my every movement
Crippling me
I don't want to be here
I don't want to be anywhere
I disrespect the fabric of my family's reality
Like a petulant fool
At every ill turn of a winding road
That leads to nowhere

And I am so, so sorry

There is fuck all in your future
When you are drinking yourself to death

I am too honest, it defeats me
Yet still, I cannot stop crying, balling
Dining on my inability
My absolute, resolute, cannot do this
My nature is to object to help
I cannot handle it
Leave me alone, unholy machine,
Moloch's Howl
Begone!

My refusal to stop suddenly, sober
Like last time
And go stark raving mad
To try to end my life
With a fistful of pills and a well of hopeless tears
Is unbearable to me
I am trapped
I will do anything, even die a horrible death, drunk
Smiling through the piss, the black pouring rain
Just so I don't visit hell again
I would rather wither and leave this realm slowly
Painfully
Than go through all of that again

I cannot forgive myself
Let alone you

Lord of nothing
Deliver me from this torment
Church of nothing
Save me
For I cannot save myself
I cannot pray
I cannot call upon redemption
I am truly lost
I am at the bottom of a deep, dark well
And no one knows how to retrieve me

There is a ladder
There is a rope
I'd rather not utilise them, climb them
Free myself on my own

You cannot help someone
Who cannot help themselves

Love Sickness Uber Alles

A blank page
and a pen
To keep me company
A naked flame to clothe me
A shimmering tongue to illuminate my face
Dripping import atop a wasted candle
Just so I don't feel alone

I wish the words
Would write themselves
That the stone would bleed
Without me having to squeeze it
Inspiration is a distant companion
In a foreign prison
If it is indeed receiving my letters
Why doesn't it get back to me?

My mind is calloused,
The cracks are spreading
Like a cathode ray,
A pregnant tube TV,
Caged in a cranial womb
My hands shake
Like the wings of a rapacious moth
How shall I draw you in?
Pencil thin?

I wish these pages
Would turn themselves
I wish these words
Would read themselves

Perhaps love
Does not wish to be described?
Can't someone else
Pad the walls of the asylum?
Let me rest in your violent silence

A blank page
and a pen
To keep me safe and warm
To keep me from bombing out on the horizon
To gift me solace from your storm

My edible, breakable mind
In the kitchen of an enthusiastic cannibal
Deserving of their own cable cooking show
Fragile, and so human
Faint from traversing the labyrinth
Of your heart

I can still hear you in the distance
Yet I cannot find you
Are you hiding?
Do you even want to be found?

Your exquisite kiss
Would be the last thing
I would ever taste

Please think for me
Please feel for me
Please kill for me

I can't bear to…

Spiders and Vampires

Death crawls all over me
A thousand angry spiders
There is no brushing them away
They're here to stay

And all I can think is
I've given up on romance
The spiders love me
Death loves me
That's all that matters

Hire me an undead prostitute or a vampire
Either way
I will possess love
And it will possess me
Blood, extracted by kissing, slurping, sucking
Poison, injected via fangs, bites
There are dirty spiders in my blood
Rotting teeth biting into my heart
Drink me, devour me, deflower me
Write me into oblivion
I am enslaved by arachnids and haemoglobin

The regal vampire, an empire
Dressed to kill
The morbid spiders
Hungering to puncture flesh
And poison the mind

In 'n' out, in 'n' out, in 'n' out
Venom and blood
Venom in
Blood out
Fuck me and call me Jesus,
Virgin Mary
Sink your fangs into my heart
Bleed me out, blot me out, disbelieve me
Give me religion and feed me bourbon
Test me till I fail
Bleach me till I bail
Eviscerate me, hollow me, pray for me
I am unsavable

I'll do whatever you want
I'll be whoever you want
I am your test store dummy
I am your losing score

Just remember
That
Once upon a time
I saved you

Just forget
All the horrible things I did
In order to seduce you

Give me a free pass, please
Coz I am so fucking sorry, lazy, crazy
Allow me to spasm into the chasm
Of your choosing, hell hound, bitch, beloved dog
If you're going to banish me to an island
Let it be an island of my choosing
If you're going to reject me
Let me decide the locale, the geo-pornography
Of my prison

You can't fuck me, beloved bitch
For I am unfuckable

The Freedom from Information Act

Freedom from information
If you want to know
Why the chicken crossed the road
There's no point
Asking the chicken
It doesn't know
Sometimes people just act
Without knowing why

Freedom from love
Freedom from sex
Freedom from conforming
To someone else's idea
Of what it means to be human
Don't ask me how I arrived
On the other side of the road
I'm a chicken
And have absolutely no idea
How I got here

If I keep crossing this road
I will eventually, inevitably
Be hit by a passing car
And I wouldn't have it any other way
Another random act
Of senseless violence
Perhaps we should ask
The driver of the Mazda
Why he gleefully mowed me down
But he probably doesn't know either
We just do things
Without knowing why

The freedom from information
It's an act
It's an ad
Just don't do it

Insert Coin

What do you do,
When the wall hits you?
What do you do,
When the line crosses you?

Answer:

A fist full of pharmaceuticals
A white-knuckled blackout
Of pretty pills
If you're happy and you know it
Take your meds
(All of them)

Sorry
If my attempted suicide
Inconvenienced you
I guess date night
Will have to be rescheduled
Doctors, nurses and devils
All angered by my imperceptible desire
To die
Three days in the ICU
Strapped to dozens of bleeping machines
It was a close call, a shambolic frenzy
To keep my heart beating
I failed, thank fuck
I guess I'm not an overachiever
After all

Death says,

'The point of suicide should be to succeed
Successful people die by this principle'

Don't leave Death lingering
Grasp life by both testicles, twist, and then let them go
There is no place in the advertised apocalypse
For cowards and sycophants

Now there is a distinct disconnect
Between my eyes and my brain
I am seeing things
I shouldn't be able to see
Like you
In a blood-soaked wedding dress
Scoffing personality pills
From a belching vending machine
Like you
With a buzzing chainsaw
In one hand
And a Get Out of Jail Free card
In the other

Insert coin
Ad nauseam
Again, and again
Happiness is a warm, glowing slot machine
Vivisection is the special creature feature

The elevator has stopped between floors
You have a captive audience
Like you
They are trapped
In a poorly ventilated purgatory
Pressing every single button
Till they're all lit up
Like mesmerised eyes
In an auditorium, a stadium, a dirty bathroom stall
Like you
Letting one rip in an overcrowded coffin
Everyone else gasps for unsullied air
No one here gets out alive

Like me
Pregnant face and expectant cheeks
My eyes like drooping tits
Weeping shadow milk
Sweeping up the leaves you left behind
In the middle of a hurricane

It's all I have left to remember us by
A mental photo album of memories
Rescued from floodwaters
Pages faded, bloated and bleached of colour
Like you, cremating history
Rewriting the truth
In some demented, foggy yesterday
Covered in contusions and sipping champagne
Staring back from the page
Eyeballing me
Mouthing every word that I write
Sucking ink from my pen
Like liquid soul from a withered groin

You're out of coins
The machine is no longer purring
The elevator is finally moving
When the doors creep open
You'll be on your own
And everything will return
To abnormal

Like me
It's not like you
At all

Sell Me Why I'm Here

Can someone sell me why I'm here
In this coffin
Six feet underground
Buried alive, still breathing
For now
I'm beginning to regret
Faking my own death
Getting through the funeral
Was an ordeal
Performance art is not my forte
Still, I feigned not breathing
I didn't move, twitch or itch
I deceived everyone

The plan was to burst out of my open casket
Look everyone in the eye
Raise a middle finger
And smile
Like I'd accomplished something remarkable
Like I was merely pretending
Like I truly was an insufferable prick
With a terrible sense of humour
And I wasn't going anywhere
Not yet
Like the lack of emotion and grief
The formality
The insanity
Had been worth it
Just to catch everyone in the act
Of not caring much that I was gone

Unfortunately, I fell asleep
At the most inopportune time
I slept through the eulogy
I slept through the burial
You'd think my snoring would have given me away

Can someone tell me why I'm here
I know it's my own fault
It wasn't meant to end this way
Thrashing about
Bashing at the walls of my tomb
Screaming
Just so someone might hear
It's so dark
The air is retreating
But then an eerie sense of calm
Washes over me
I am resigned to my fate
In life, sometimes an elaborate joke
Is the very thing that kills you

I'm wondering if I should have gone
With cremation instead
But how do you fake that?

The Power of Disco

The lucky ones come to God
Through the power of Disco
So, if you have a Saturday Night Fever
Say your prayers
And take some paracetamol

Those less fortunate come to God
Through Folk and Country

The damned, those that never made it
Into the lecherous arms of the three-pronged trinity
Were seduced by Rock 'n' Roll
The devil never sounded so persuasive
Nor his arguments so delicious and damnable

Pop and R 'n' B don't matter
But they are a way to pass the time
Hip Hop and Rap are mostly crap
But there are rare moments
When even God looks fondly
Upon his most abominable creations

Celine Dion, Mariah Carey, Christina Aguilera
All the Divas are believers
And that's why they're going to hell

Purgatory, populated as it is by Jazz
Is neither here nor there, literally

Gospel was never going to fool or convert anyone

Techno and Dance
Is for atheists and ecstasy takers
Their high is your low
Their glow stick is your lightsaber
And the force is strong

Thrash, Death and Black Metal
That's where you hear the Antichrist in action
He's an ambitious bastard,
Radio play is not part of his plan
Neither is your redemption

Heavy Metal was created by God
Leather, studs and long hair
Homoeroticism is the surest way into heaven
Have you peered at Christ, naked on that cross?
That loin cloth, only just obscuring the groin of God
It just so happens, and so it seems
That when Heavy Metal happened
God was a closeted homosexual teen

The Blues?
Played by Satan himself, a black deity,
to a standing ovation
and a post abortion ovulation
With guitar strings that could hang a man
Plucked straight from the unholy swamps of Louisiana

I'm Thinking of Leaving You

She pretends she's in love
She administers old, ratty socks to her feet
Like holy prophylactics
It's cold
But everything is cold
In and out of the seasons
That shape our desires
She pretends to enjoy making love
But he's just too agreeable
He goes down on her
Like he's an eager to please puppy dog
His tongue is like bad literature
Always descriptive
Never getting to the point
That would give her satisfaction
He's missing the point
And only she knows it

He pretends that she loves him
But deep down he knows
Imagining walks in the rain
Where the wetness doesn't matter
Like a moist vagina, now dry from disinterest
Where getting soaked is romantic
Where their hands touch
Where the tactile matters
So much
And someone's heart is breaking
In the downpour
But whose?

It makes him sad to know
She doesn't really care for him
He studies her face
Like a forgery of some Dorian Grey Renoir
He imagines
That there is a painting of her
Elsewhere
That reveals her as she truly is
Perhaps her beauty is a lie
Is he masturbating to a portrait?
When he lies in bed at night
Is it her that he truly sees?

She fakes every orgasm
What she doesn't realise
Is that he's faking it too
Without a relatable connection
He feels nothing
He's just hoping
She'll come around
He implodes
Rather than explodes
Inside of her
She feigns pleasure
Neither of them
Know any other recourse
To a love that isn't love, defying emotion
Or tender connection

They discuss Nietzsche, Albert Camus
Bukowski, Dali, Antonin Artaud
The state of world politics
Covid 19, the latest Academy Award
They can't believe it's not margarine
Asteroids could hit the earth
At any given time
They talk about generational terrorism
But none of it is a threat
To them
In their hyper reality bubble
It may as well be real
But it isn't

None of it matters
They make love
Although those aren't the correct words
Rather, they fuck like strangers
That know each other too unwell
Perhaps that's where love fails
Mismatched in the heat of passion
Neither knowing the other
Who among them could be bothered
When their empathy
Amounts to indifferent equality

Who can really tell
Whether they should be together
Sometimes the simple act of lovemaking
Says more
Than any love poem
Could possibly explain

And the sadness swallows us whole

www.ingramcontent.com/pod-product-compliance
Lightning Source LLC
Chambersburg PA
CBHW070944080526
44587CB00015B/2216